"KiD STUFF"

253 QUOTES BY THE YOUNGER "SET"
AT HOME • SUNDAY SCHOOL • PLAY •
AND WHEREVER YOU FIND THEM

Compiled by Eleanor L. Doan

from Gospel Light's "Teach" magazine

Designed by Joyce Thimsen

G/L
REGAL
BOOKS
TM

A Division of G/L Publications
Glendale, California, U.S.A.

ACKNOWLEDGMENT

Grateful acknowledgment is due to the scores
of parents, grandparents, Sunday School teachers
and friends of the "younger set" who contributed
these charming quotes—and sometimes misquotes—
to *Teach* Magazine. We are sharing them
again, this time in a single collection, for
your personal enjoyment, use as illustrations,
examples, attention getters . . . and because
wisdom from the mouth of babes can be
profitable to grownups!

Published by
Regal Book Divisions, G/L Publications
Glendale, California 91209, U.S.A.

Library of Congress Catalog No.: 77-122884
ISBN O-8307-0085-4

Contents

Kids are FRANK

At Christmas time a mother and her tiny tot daughter found themselves involved in a rather confusing discussion about angels. Finally, in despair at not being able to answer her daughter's questions, the mother said: "I know what let's do. Let's ask our minister."

"Why should we ask him?" said the little girl. "What does he know about it? He's no angel!"

R. A. Morrison, Fresno, Calif.

Kim knelt by his bed with his mother to pray. Suddenly he began to call, "Mother! Mother!"

Mother only replied, "We're praying, tell me later." When they finished, mother asked Kim, "What was wrong?"

"Nothing now," said Kim, "but you were kneeling on my fingers."

Marilyn Miller, Roaring Spring, Pa.

1

It was my morning on duty at our church day school, and an early morning home shampoo had left my naturally curly hair completely unmanageable. As the children appeared on the playground we exchanged our usual happy greeting, until Cathy, a very observant and forthright little girl, skipped up, looked at me for a moment and sweetly quipped,

"Teacher, don't feel bad. This morning my mommie didn't have time to comb my hair either!"

E. Margueritte Baker, San Bernardino, Calif.

Greg listened attentively as I explained to my Sunday school class how important it is to ask God's blessing upon our meals.

"Greg," I asked, "don't you think the blessing makes the food taste better?"

"Well," he answered, "it may help some things, but it sure don't do much for stew!"

Bonnie Wegner, Minneapolis, Minn.

The mother of a four-year-old child who had a substitute Sunday school teacher asked, "What do you think of your new teacher?"

"Oh, she's smarter than Miss Smith. When she played the piano she used one finger. When Miss Smith plays she has to use two hands."

Ola A. Pool, No. Hollywood, Calif.

"Must I keep pounding this thing? The noise is giving me a headache!"

Joan Miller, Chicago, Ill.

3

Daddy asked six-year-old Cindy to get something for him, and she replied, "I don't want to!"

"I am the boss and you are to get it," said Daddy.

"Okay," said Cindy, and she went to get the item. As she handed it to her father, she had the last word. "Good Christian Daddies usually say thank you."

Mary Sheriff, Seattle, Wash.

There was a great deal of discussion around home and school while my mother was deciding whether to move from a teaching position in Indiana to one in New York. She almost stayed in Indiana when she heard one of her third grade boys say:

"But she just can't go, Mother. Next to Jesus, she's my best friend."

Mrs. T. J. Kleinhaus, Biloxi, Mississippi

Guests were visiting for Sunday dinner, and Marty had embarrassed her mother by misbehaving. Her punishment was to eat her dinner alone at a small table in the corner of the dining room.

The rest of the family and guests paid little attention to her until they heard her saying grace before eating: "I thank Thee, Lord, for preparing a table before me in the presence of mine enemies."

T. M. Pendergrass, Tucumcari, New Mexico

"Personally, I think Mr. Haver's carrying this visual aid thing a little too far!"

Six-year-old Greg answered a question in Sunday school class. His teacher said, "You must have a good Mommy to tell you about God and things in the Bible."

"She doesn't have to," replied Greg. "I learn enough about that at church."

Irene Royce, White Lake, Wis.

Baby-sitting with five-year-old Sharon was anything but boring. She could think up ideas twice as fast as I could talk her out of them.

One of our more peaceful evenings was partially spent in cutting pictures from a catalog (probably a new one!). She handed me a pair of scissors with the command to help.

Then, carefully inspecting the first picture I had cut out, Sharon gave her verdict: "You do good for your age."

Irene Royce, White Lake, Wis.

Our family was on a day-long car trip, and after lunch I offered to drive and give father a little rest. From the back seat four-year-old Harvey asked, "Are you going to drive, Mom?"

"Yes," I replied. After a brief moment of reflection, Harvey advised gravely, "Mom, I think you better pray."

Mrs. Mary Rempel, Mission City, B.C.

"Dear God, please help my Sunday school teacher to be able to get along without me this morning!"

Mrs. Iris Eldredge, San Gabriel, California

The Presbyterian minister had been summoned to the bedside of a Methodist woman who was very ill. As he went up the walk, he met the little daughter and said to her, "I am very glad your mother called for me in her illness. Is your minister out of town?"

"No," answered the child. "He's at home, but we thought Mother might have something contagious and we didn't want to expose him to it."

I visited an open house at an elementary school and one 5th grade teacher displayed papers written by her pupils on the topic: "What Is a Teacher?"

One boy wrote: "Teachers are usually women because it seems women are smarter than men. But some men are teachers."

Members of our family differed on the candidates in the recent presidential election. During one get-together the argument got especially heated and my mother-in-law sought to inject a lighter tone by turning to my three-year-old son and asking, "Michael, who are you for? Nixon or Kennedy?"

Michael's reply was quick and positive: "I'm for Jesus."

Mrs. Robert Flack, La Crescenta, Calif.

The pastor visited the Sunday evening youth group and volunteers were called on to pray. Little Bonnie volunteered to pray for the pastor. Her prayer: "Be with our pastor and help him to preach a better sermon next Sunday."

Viola Anderson, Humboldt, Ia.

9

Kids are HELPFUL

My young daughter was a lover of nature at an early age. One day after a rainstorm when she was two years old, I saw her riding up and down the sidewalk on her tricycle with several long angle worms draped over the handle bars. When I asked her what she was doing, her reply was, "I'm taking my friends for a ride."

Mrs. Wm. Greig Jr., Glendale, Calif.

At a dinner one evening I was relating to my wife some problems that had come up at a recent meeting of Christian Education Directors. One of the problems mentioned was: "How can you wake up the people in a dead church?"

Three of our young children offered solutions from their own limited experience. Our six-year-old said, "Use an alarm clock!" Our four-year-old suggested, "You could sqweam!" And our seven-year-old clinched it by saying: "Drop all of the offering money on the floor!"

Mr. Michael McCourt, Alderwood Manor, Washington

In Sunday school we were discussing which day would be the best day to have the Sunday school picnic. I asked Donald, a young boy from a quite distant farm, which day would be best for him.

In all sincerity he replied, "My father will let me go ANY day it rains."

Miss Edna Elsaser, Boonville, New York

A mother registering her small son in kindergarten for the first time was informed that proof of age was necessary for registration. She agreed to send his birth certificate along the following Sunday.

Next Sunday morning the youngest appeared with the required document and the comment, "Here's my excuse for being born."

Mrs. Adele Ashley, Fontana, Calif.

11

After the mad rush of getting the older children ready for a party and putting the young ones to bed for a nap, a harried mother rested her aching head on the cool kitchen table. At this point, she felt her four-year-old's hand on her shoulder. "What's the matter, Mommy?" he asked sympathetically. "Don't you have anything to do?"

On the day after Christmas, my five-year-old nephew Roy went with his parents to a ski resort in Washington State. The family, who had not made advance reservations, went to the desk to inquire about accommodations.

The clerk spent a long time looking at his book and going through cards, and finally said, "I'm awfully sorry, but we have no space available."

Before anyone could reply, Roy, standing on his toes so that he could see over the desk, said, "Well, do you have a manger?"

PS: The hotel clerk looked again at his books and found accommodations for the family.

Doris Gray, New York, N.Y.

Little Janie came into the house and told her mother that her friend Susie had dropped her doll and it had broken.

"Did you help her fix it?" Janie's mother asked.

"No, we couldn't fix it," Janie replied, "but I helped her cry."

Mrs. C. J. Hallman, Bergen, Alberta

"No, I don't need you to ride shotgun!"

14

I once taught in a mission Sunday school located in a rough mountain community. One Sunday I was having particular difficulty in quieting my restless class of seven- and eight-year-olds. After several futile attempts, I received unexpected help from one of the little girls who matter-of-factly stated, "And we gotta marry those guys!"

The boys were remarkably quiet during the remaining part of the lesson.

Eunice Braun, Abbotsford, B.C.

Two of our little girls were playing in the front yard. The older girl had several loose baby teeth and Mary Ann accidentally knocked one of them out. Sharon came into the kitchen and laid her tooth on the white tile sink while she used several gallons of water to rinse out her mouth. I was busy wiping up the sink and didn't notice, but apparently the tooth floated on down the drain.

When Sharon looked for her tooth to put under her pillow for the good fairy to exchange for a small amount of cash, and discovered that it was gone, she started to cry. Mary Ann felt sorry for her and said, "Don't cry, Sharon. Come on outside and I'll knock another tooth out for you."

Mary Ann Lamascus, Downey, Calif.

It was a late spring afternoon, and our twins, age six, found a baby bird that had fallen out of the nest. They tried to help the little bird "get well" but were unsuccessful. They dug a hole to bury it, and had some cuttings from shrubs to line the grave, when Shannon suddenly jumped up.

"Wait, Sharon," he said. "I want to get some tissue paper to wrap the little bird in so the angels won't get their hands dirty when they come to get it."

Mary Ann Lamascus, Downey, Calif.

"Hurry up, Danny! I'm holding the bus for you!"

Kids are IMAGINATIVE

My six-year-old boys were making clay models of baby Moses in a basket. I looked at each one when they were completed, and made some encouraging comment. When I came to Richard's model I noticed an extra strip of clay across the top of the basket, and asked him what it was. "Oh, that's his seat belt!" came the reply.

Brady Evans, Chicago, Ill.

"My drawing of the Red Sea is blank because the Israelites are gone over, and the Egyptians are drowned."

Five-year-old Debbie was helping me review the story of the ten lepers. When she came to the part where only the ONE leper came back to thank Jesus, she hesitated. Trying to help her remember I said, "And what did Jesus say to the ONE that DID come back to thank HIM?" She thought a minute and then with a sweet smile answered: "You're welcome?"

Mrs. Lucille Farina, Chicago, Illinois

My Primary class gave an impromptu play in which Joseph and the butler were discussing their reasons for being in prison:

"Potiphar's wife told tales on me," said Joseph. "What did you do?"

"Oh, I turned the wine into water," replied the butler.

Mrs. C. E. Moffitt, Central Tilba, N.S.W., Australia

One school morning as I tried for the second or third time to awaken my six-year-old son, he half-opened his eyes, looked at me in disgust, and remarked, "Whoever invented morning sure made it too early."

Mrs. Jacqueline Ahlstrand, Cupertine, Calif.

"Reverend Brown says, we can do without 'Three Blind Mice' if you don't mind."

20

The new Sunday school teacher had finished a lesson on the Ten Commandments and was rather pleased with the children's response. "And now," she said, "let's have a memory test. Who can recite a commandment that has only four words in it?"

A hand shot up immediately.

"Yes, Paul?" said the teacher.

"Keep off the grass."

Roy Nourse, Seattle, Wash.

Ten-year-old Billy was admiring the night sky. There on the desert away from city lights the sky was so black, and there were so many stars visible that Billy commented, "It looks like dandruff."

Wm. Greig Jr., Glendale, Calif.

"I bet that librarian will remember my impromptu drum solo for as long as she lives."

Kids are IMITATIVE

Nathan was being especially noisy in class one morning. Hoping to quiet him, his teacher said, "Nathan, you shouldn't talk so loudly in church."

Nathan looked at her and replied, "Billy Graham does."

Marjorie Soderholm, Chicago, Ill.

A radio announcer's small son was overheard saying his bedtime prayers. He prayed in a conventional manner until he came to the end, ". . . and God bless all the boys and girls of the world, and be with all the missionaries around the world.

"In Jesus' name, Amen and *FM!*"

Mrs. Phil Nordlund, Tacoma, Wash.

At least one impression of Daddy's preaching has registered with our nursery age daughter. She has been observed pounding books and Bibles, waving her arms, and shouting for all she is worth.

Amos Clemmons, Saugus, Calif.

"This morning we will preach the gossip."

Kids are INQUISITIVE

I was teaching my kindergarteners about how God sent the ravens to feed Elijah with bread and meat, when one little girl looked up in surprise and asked, "No catsup?"

Mrs. G. H. Martz, Emmett, Idaho

Nine-year-old Tommy was causing a disturbance in Sunday school. His teacher, a spinster of middle age, spoke to him a second time and Tommy reluctantly promised to behave. Still not sure that he would be good, the teacher said, "Yes, but I know boys."

Tommy looked up and replied, "Is that why you never married one?"

Ada Noble, Barrhead, Alberta

At ground-breaking ceremonies for the new Church Education Building, five-year-old Kenny was an interested spectator. As the minister solemnly removed a spadeful of earth, Kenny inquired in a loud stage whisper, "Daddy, are they going to put the building in that hole?"

Mrs. Harold Casper, Merchantville, N.J.

The Sunday school superintendent had just brought the attendance book to the teacher. On leaving the room, he leaned over to the teacher, whispering an invitation to her and her husband to come to his house for coffee that evening.

After the superintendent had left, a little boy said, "What's he trying to do, make a date with you?"

Mrs. C. D. Skinner, Dallas, Texas

As I told the Bible story, little Tommy sat in rapt attention, eyes never leaving my face. Thrilled at such rapport, I felt that the Lord surely must be speaking to him. At the close of the story I asked, "Now, boys and girls, are there any questions?"

Tommy's hand shot up.

"All right, Tommy, what would you like to ask?"

"Teacher, what makes your mouth go crooked when you talk?"

Mrs. Helen Cramer, Pacoima, Calif.

The family was preparing to go to the mission field, and each person had to receive several shots. Finally little Janie asked her mother, "Mommie, do you have to get a shot to go to heaven?"

Mrs. Earl Carter, Pekin, Illinois

Kids are LITERAL

A primary boy was upset, and the teacher asked him what was the matter. He said, "The preacher is dead." The teacher was surprised and said, "He's not dead, where did you get that idea?" The little boy replied, "Well, they prayed last Sunday in church that he would have a safe trip to the Holy Land."

Jane Ellis, Jackson, Miss.

The first year I helped with VBS, we took roll by asking each child to answer, "Present." When his name was called, one little boy replied, "I don't have a present tonight, but I will bring one tomorrow night."

It was hard to finish roll call.

Mrs. Paul Keckler, Waynesboro, Pa.

Three-year-old Dale sat "writing" with pencil and paper while Mother fed the baby.

"Mama, what this for?" he asked, pointing to the pencil's eraser.

"When you make a mistake, that's what you use to rub it out."

Dale went back to marking on the paper, but soon looked up and asked, "Mama, how do you make a mistake?"

Margaret E. Brown, Tecate, Calif.

Six-year-old Gary recited his memory verse perfectly, but the teacher also urged him to give the reference.

"It's in the book of Hatchet," Gary decided.

The mystery was finally solved when one knowing little girl informed everyone, "He means Ax." (Acts)

Roberta Lashley, Elmira, New York

Five-year-old Billy who had gone to Sunday school with a nickel for offering surprised his family on the way home from church by announcing, "I've got lotsa money now!" And for proof he emptied his pockets, revealing one nickel, one dime, and three pennies.

"Billy, you tell me exactly where that money came from," demanded the boy's father.

"Sure, Daddy," answered Billy. "I got it at Sunday school. The teacher said, 'Let's take the offering,' so I did!"

A thoughtful aunt of mine volunteered to take a neighborhood child to church for the first time. The child was awed by the service and full of questions.

When a newborn was presented for baptism, the child seemed puzzled. "The parents are giving the baby to God," explained my aunt.

Seeing the minister return the baby to its parents the youngster commented matter-of-factly, "Guess God didn't want *that* one."

Mrs. Judie Underwood, St. Louis, Missouri

Our first grader, Sarah, was having difficulty understanding the moral of a story she'd heard at school. After one truly first grade exasperating day, Sarah told her mother, "Mommie, I'm having a problem at school. I'm having trouble with my morals." And her father is a minister!

Max R. Hickerson, Cincinnati, Ohio

The beginners were joyfully singing, and between songs the teacher asked, "How many sing when they are happy?"

One little five-year-old sparkled, "I sing all the time, I even sing in bed!"

This pleased the teacher so much that she asked the class, "How many sing in bed?"

At that, a little golden-haired miss seriously exclaimed, "I don't know that song!"

Ethel Lake, Granada Hills, Calif.

30

"Mommie, was it really a 'bomb'?"

Mrs. Alta B. Calkins, San Ysidro, California

31

Six-year-old Luther listened attentively during bedtime devotions while Daddy read the little card Luther had picked for his Scripture treasure that night: *He that spareth his rod hateth his son: but he that loveth him chasteneth him.* The reading was followed by an explanation: "Daddy sometimes has to punish but he does it in love."

After prayers and goodnights all was quiet for some time. Then from the darkness came a small voice: "Daddy . . ."

"Yes, what is it, Luther?"

"I wish you didn't love me *quite* so *hard* sometimes."

Lois P. Brown, Elmhurst, Ill.

Six-year-old Brian returned from vacation enchanted with the fact that he had gone fishing. "What kind of fish did you catch?" his Sunday school teacher asked. "Stink fish," Brian replied. Puzzled, the teacher later asked Brian's father what kind of fish were called "stink" fish. To her amusement he replied, "Not stink fish. We caught smelt!"

Rosa Blandford, Glendale, California

A kindergarten boy didn't want to put his money in the offering plate.

"If I were you, I'd put my money in the plate," encouraged his teacher.

The reluctant giver replied, "If *you* want to put *your* money in the offering plate, put it in."

Connie Ritter, Richfield, Pa.

Going home from Sunday school I asked my rather bashful four-year-old what he did in class that day. Seriously he replied, "My teacher tells us all to say 'present'; but we never get any."

Mrs. Roland Rush, Levant, Kansas

Five-year-old Timmy thrust his Sunday school paper into Mother's hand.

"Today Miss Ginny told us about Jesus who died on the cross."

His mother nodded. "That's why we have Easter," she said.

Timmy pointed to the picture of the crucifixion. "Who are all those people standing there?"

His mother replied, "The people who loved Jesus."

Timmy looked at the picture a moment. Then he said, "Which one is Miss Ginny?"

Mrs. Catharine Brandt, St. Paul, Minn.

It was Promotion Sunday in our church. Wondering how much my primary class understood about this concept, I asked, "Who can tell me what special day this is?"

Without hesitation one bright-eyed youngster said, "I know! I know! It's COMMOTION SUNDAY!"

Mrs. F. W. Roseburg, Isle, Minn.

34

My missionary husband had long trusted God to supply the needs of our family of eight children. Sometimes the "day-old" bread had to be made into bread pudding, and the "yesterday's" donuts had to be reheated, but God always saw us through.

One day our five-year-old daughter concluded her table grace prayer by thanking God for the food and asking Him to ". . . bless those who repaired it!"

Mrs. R. Owens, Paramount, Calif.

Little Howard had a hot temper and often used brash words. His Sunday school teacher told him, "You should always give a soft answer when you get angry or something annoys you." Howard promised he would try. Soon Howard's younger brother began to tease. Clenching his fist in rage Howard started to go after his brother, then stopped and said: "Oh, mush!"

Evelyn Pleyer, Medford, Ore.

One Sunday during our vacation we decided to visit the church of our former pastor, an inner city church which was integrated. Because this would be a new experience for our children, I carefully explained at breakfast that morning that in their Sunday school class there would be colored children. But Jesus loved all the children, no matter what color their skin. After church, our five-year-old Becky was in tears when she explained: "But Mother, there weren't any colored children. Just black ones and white ones."

Mrs. George A. Till, Burbank, Calif.

I asked my class of juniors to define a miracle. One ten-year-old boy said, "Well, a miracle is something no one really believes could happen—like when my mother tells me to wash my hands and face, and I wash behind my ears, too! That's a miracle."

Mrs. Ethel Roberts, Oakland, Calif.

As they crawled beneath the sheets one evening, my six-year-old daughter Karen said to her sister, "Cheryl, do you have peace in your heart?"

Astonished, I asked, "What does that mean, Karen?"

"Well," she said, "You have a heart, and there's a piece of Jesus in it."

Mrs. Jake Leis Jr., Gering, Neb.

Kids are LOGICAL

"Always remember we are here to help others," said a mother as she explained the Golden Rule.

Her little one meditated for a moment and inquired, "Well, what are the others here for?"

When my wife and I pray during family devotions, occasionally we end our prayers with the sentence, "We ask these things with thanksgiving in Jesus' Name."

One morning, Donna, our five-year-old daughter, came to the end of her prayer and closed with this rejoinder: "We ask these things with Thanksgiving and Christmas and Easter in Jesus' Name."

David R. Enlow, Chicago, Illinois

Four-year-old Eddy fixed his eyes on the Sunday school teacher as she told how we get our bread:

"First, the farmer sows his seed, then God sends rain and sunshine. The grain is harvested and ground into flour. Then the baker makes the flour into loaves of bread."

Eddy could wait no longer. "Maybe some get theirs that way," he said, "but we get our bread at Casey's Store."

Mrs. Alice M. Dubler, Manchester, N.Y.

A first grader told her teacher that she was one of eight children. "My, but it must be expensive to have so many children," the teacher said.

"Oh," said the child, "we don't buy them; we just raise them."

Transportation is at a premium in the town where I am a pastor and I often give members of my congregation a lift home after church. One Sunday I heard the following conversation in the back seat:

"Give me some money to stop at the store," a little girl asked her brother.

"I don't have any," was the reply.

"I don't have any either," I chimed in, half in fun.

"You ought to," the little girl told me, "I gave you some."

Rev. Georgia Byrd, Milledgeville, Ga.

"I didn't know angels had to rehearse."

39

My five-year-old neighbor taught me very effectively that patience and "listenability" are true virtues. As I dressed hurriedly for an evening meeting, he chatted aimlessly and endlessly.

But he did insist on knowing where I was going. Finally, in desperation and exasperation, I blurted out, "Nowhere, Billy, nowhere!"

Out of the corner of my eye I saw him scratch his head skeptically. "But," he replied thoughtfully, "where will you be when you get there?"

Bernard A. Shepard, Santa Cruz, California

Conversation heard between two small boys in Sunday school:

"Are you a Junior or Primary?"

"I don't know."

"Do girls bother you?"

"No."

"You're a Primary."

The teacher was telling her first graders how dark and awful it must have been for Jonah in the stomach of the whale.

"What do you think Jonah did down there?" she queried, expecting someone to answer that he must have prayed.

From a serious little boy came the reply: "He lit a match."

Miss Mae Mouland, Fort William, Ont., Can.

One day my five-year-old son burst through the kitchen door sobbing because his playmates had been teasing him about his freckles. I told him that God loved him very much just the way he was and that his freckles were undoubtedly God's kisses.

A few weeks later he slammed in the back door holding a bright orange tiger lily and exclaimed excitedly, "Look, Mummy, I've found something else that has God's special speckles on its face too!"

Nadene M. Murphy, Valemount, B.C.

The superintendent, coming into the classroom of beginners and finding it noisy, rang the bell for silence. When the room was quiet, she asked, "What do we do when we come into the house of the Lord?"

One four-year-old answered, "Open the door."

Mrs. John C. Lewis, Revere, Mass.

We were talking about Christian compassion so I asked my third grade class if they didn't feel sorrow when their brothers were sad. "If you see your brother crying, don't you feel sorry, too?" I asked an angelic eight-year-old.

She considered this gravely, tossing her blonde curls. "No, I really don't," she replied, "because if my brother is crying it's usually because I've just hit him."

Patricia Paden, Needham Heights, Mass.

During a summer storm, the family stood anxiously watching the clouds, wondering if damage would be done to their crops. When the rain seemed to have passed over without the expected hail, Mother was much relieved.

"Good," she sighed, "it's gone south."

Four-year-old Susan wonderingly piped up, "Mother, doesn't anyone live down south?"

Miss Ada Noble, Alberta, Canada

Jay's mother was losing patience. "Your room is a mess," she said to her ten-year-old. "Clean it up or I'm taking ten cents off your allowance." An hour later she looked in on him and scolded, "You haven't cleaned the room! Now I'm going to take ten cents more off."

"But Mom, that's not fair," Jay protested. "It's the same mess."

Laura Edwards Russ, Glasser, New Jersey

42

"Maybe it comes naturally, with the fifteen-year pin."

The teacher was giving her 4th-grade girls a lesson on Abraham and Sarah having as many children as the sands on the seashore and the stars in the heavens. Teacher explained that this meant that "their children's children would number this many."

Cynthia raised her hand and exclaimed, "Oh, I'm glad to hear that. I was thinking Sarah would have to be in the hospital a real long time for all those children!"

Mrs. Margie Gray, Downey, Calif.

My daughter is a pupil in my first grade class. After studying Noah and his family, I asked if someone could name Noah's sons.

Up went my daughter's hand: "Shem, Ham, and Bacon!"

The following Sunday we were studying Abraham, and I asked for the name of Abraham's wife, hinting that it began with "S."

My daughter had another meaty answer ready: "Steak!"

Mrs. Howard Reed, Milan, Mich.

Kids are PRACTICAL

After studying Jonah's life and what it means to be a missionary, I had my sixth grade boys write postcards to their friends inviting them to Sunday school. When checking the cards before mailing, I came upon this message:

"Dear Mike, come to Sunday school with me next week or I'll knock you flat. Tom."

Mrs. Norman Dixon, Raynham, Mass.

I suggested to our four-year-old Paul we make a beautiful birthday cake for Jesus and put a candle on it this Christmas. He was most enthusiastic, but became troubled, asking me, "How would we get it up there?"

Mrs. Charles D. Hobby, Tacoma, Wash.

One evening Johnny's mother told him to get the mop from outside. He said, "I'm afraid of the dark." His mother told him not to be afraid, because Jesus was everywhere and that he would be protected.

Little Johnny timidly opened the door and, looking out into the black night, he said, "Jesus, please hand me the mop."

Inise Meeker, Pryor, Okla.

46

Little Dick, his brother, Harry, and his cousin, Malvick, were visiting Dick's grandmother, and Dick was called on to ask the blessing at dinner that night.

Said Dick: "God bless Grandma, God bless Grandpa, God bless Malvick and God bless Harry. But don't bless me, because I can take care of myself."

A little girl trying hard to explain heaven to her friend finally asked in desperation, "Don't you want to go to heaven with me?"

"Well, sure," replied her little friend, "but I can't today. Mom said I was supposed to come home right after Sunday school!"

Mr. and Mrs. Lonnie Brigham, Redding, California

The Primary Church leader was conducting a discussion on being kind to others by sharing. To "nail her point down," she said, "Suppose you had just finished putting a model plane together and a friend came over and wanted to fly it. What would you do?"

Several children gave answers that indicated they knew they *should* let the friend have a turn, but it was obvious they weren't sure they really *would* do that. Then one little boy said, "I know what you could do! You could say the glue wasn't dry yet!"

Frances Blankenbaker, San Gabriel, Calif.

My six-year-old daughter had worked all week on committing her memory verse so she could repeat it for her teacher in Sunday school. On Sunday afternoon I asked her if she had said her memory verse.

She said, "No, I couldn't."

"Why not?" I asked.

She replied, "All I'd get was a balloon."

Mrs. Roy Hicks, Omaha, Neb.

The Sunday school teacher was teaching the beginners to give sentence prayers of thankfulness. When Ellen's turn came, she was silent. The teacher leaned over and whispered, "Ellen, why don't you tell God you are thankful for good health?"

Still more silence. Finally Ellen spoke up, "I just can't. I've had a stomach ache all morning."

Mrs. Julius M. Hovan, Parksville, Ky.

Try as I would, I couldn't get my primary students to pray in a natural manner. "Just talk to Jesus like you would to a friend," I urged. "David, will you pray out loud today?"

There was such a long pause I thought he hadn't heard me. Suddenly he blurted, "Hey, God, d'you know what?"

Mrs. Ruth Peterman, Minneapolis, Minn.

A fourth grade Sunday school boy was experiencing his first summer at the church camp. It was no time at all before his mother received his first brief but pointed letter.

"Dear Mom," it began, "please send me lots of food. All we get here is breakfast, lunch and dinner. Love, Edward."

A little girl submitted this question at our Sunday school Christmas Eve party.

"Teacher! What do you think I should give to Christ? This is really His birthday, you know."

Sydney H. Cooke, Vancouver, B.C.

The first graders had just heard the story of Baby Moses.

Teacher: "What did the Princess say when she found the baby in the basket?"

Little Girl: (with deliberate emphasis) "She said, 'Will someone go find a baby-sitter?'"

Mrs. Mildred Darrow, Lancaster, Calif.

The teacher was telling the little ones of God's care and protection—how they need never be afraid *even in the dark* because God sends His angels to watch over them. Four-year-old Randy interrupted. "But we have a night light!"

Betty Wildt, Stockton, Calif.

"Do unto others as you would like them to do unto you," remonstrated Mommy to four-year-old Joanie.

But Joanie was in no mood to be corrected.

"I don't want others to do unto me," she growled. "I want to do unto them!"

Mrs. Neil Halladay, Tarzana, Calif.

Kids are RESOURCEFUL

Judy: "Robby, where did you get that cute little puppy? Please let me hold him."

Robby: "He's our Father's Day present. If we give him to Daddy, then he will have to keep him!"

Eleanor Doan, Glendale, California

"Which one of you is having trouble seeing the chalkboard?"

". . . and when they passed the money Monte got a quarter and I got a dime!"

Seven-year-old Ronny was an enterprising young businessman. Beside his lemonade stand he had a cardboard box with a large sign reading, "For Sale, $10,000." Inside the box was a dog of mixed varieties.

After a few days the sign was gone and one of Ronny's faithful patrons asked, "Did you sell the dog, Ronny?"

"Sure did," the boy replied.

"Well, did you get $10,000 for him?" the patron asked.

"No, but I got two $5,000 kittens," the boy proudly reported.

Georgia Morton, Pacoima, Calif.

Bewildered five-year-old Johnny, who, feeling that he was lost, ran down the aisles of the supermarket shouting at the top of his lungs, "Gertrude! Gertrude! Where are you, Gertrude?"

Soon his mother, Gertrude, heard him and dried his tears.

"But you shouldn't have called me Gertrude," she chided. "You should have shouted, "Mama, Mama."

"Yeh," he sighed, "but the store is full of Mama's. I didn't think there'd be many Gertrudes."

"We brought his hammer. It keeps him quiet."

55

"Let's put him in Mrs. Allen's group. He hasn't bitten her yet."

Kids are UNPREDICTABLE

The kindly minister never lost an opportunity to help anyone in difficulty. Walking down the street, he saw a little youngster trying his best to ring a doorbell just out of reach.

"Young man, you're not quite tall enough," laughed the minister. "Let me help you," and he pushed the button.

The boy fairly tumbled down the steps shouting, "Hurry! Run before the old lady catches us!"

Doris E. Hardy, Leominster, Mass.

In telling the story of John the Baptist to a group of children, I talked at some length about baptism. When I finished, one small boy remarked, "I've never been baptized, but I was vaccinated."

Dorothy Jessup, Diagonal, Iowa

"It looks like we need another little chat about discipline."

The class was studying the return of the prodigal son story and the jealousy of his brother.

"Now let's see how well you have paid attention," said the teacher. "At the feast that was given to celebrate the return of the prodigal, there was one to whom the party brought no joy, only resentment and bitterness and disappointment. Who was it?"

A small boy raised his hand and answered with confidence, "The fatted calf."

Lucille S. Harper, Cheverly, Maryland

"Boys," I asked my class of five-year-olds, "have you ever seen someone walking on the water?"

I felt sure I would get a negative answer, but was jolted by this confident reply:

"Sure, only it had ice on."

Miss Jan Marowitch, Winnipeg, Manitoba, Can.

One little boy in my class had been especially wiggly one Sunday morning. He jumped and moved around in his chair, teased the girls near him, tapped his feet on the floor, and was totally unresponsive to everything I could think up to hold his attention.

Finally, I whispered, "Jimmy, we would like it if you could sit still for a few minutes—" Still bouncing, he replied, "I am sitting still . . . as fast as I can go!"

Betty Huey Saunders, Oswego, New York

During the worship period for our three-year-olds, the superintendent asked why God made our eyes, ears, mouth and nose. When she asked why God made our nose, one child quickly remarked, "To sneeze!"

Mary Barajikian, Hollywood, Calif.

Stephen was called upon to pray in family devotions. Just as he had mentally prepared himself for this honor, the phone near him rang. He picked up the receiver and said clearly, "Dear Heavenly Father . . ."

On the first Sunday of November, the Sunday school teacher quizzed her class of first graders.

"What special day comes this month, when we have company and eat turkey and pumpkin pie?"

Bright-eyed Rodney, just turned six, shot up his hand confidently. "Pay day," he announced.

Mrs. Bill Storlie, Vancouver, Wash.

"May I take your hat, Kent?" the Sunday school teacher asked the visitor.

"Yes," Kent replied, "but you can't have my tie!"

Frances Blankenbaker, San Gabriel, Calif.

"All I said was: 'It's such a nice day shall we hold Sunday school class outside?'"

"Oh I'm sure my Sunday school class LIKES me, Pastor. I'm just not certain they RESPECT me."

The Primary teacher had just finished a lesson in which he explained how missionaries use radio to preach the Gospel. In attempting to relate the lesson to the church's recent missions conference, he asked if the students could remember the call letters of the Sudan Interior Mission radio station in Africa (ELWA).

"The radio display was the one right by the back door of the church," he reminded the class.

"Oh, I know!" exclaimed third grader Pat. "It's EXIT!"

George Hedlund, Minneapolis, Minn.

The harassed Sunday school teacher tugged away to get a much-too-small pair of overshoes on one of her kindergarteners. Finally she succeeded, and commented, "My, but those were hard to get on!"

"Yeah," the little boy replied. "That's because they aren't mine."

Exasperated, the teacher pulled the overshoes off again.

"Well," the boy said when the overshoes were finally off, "they aren't mine—they're my brother's. But I had to wear them today."

"First of all children, I must point out some of
the rules we have at Sunday school."

Kids have EXPLANATIONS

The VBS teacher, in reviewing the previous day's lesson, asked her kindergarten students why Jesus knew the Scriptures so well. Little Richard quickly answered, "Oh, that's easy. His Daddy wrote them!"

P. R. Bunger, Los Angeles, California

On the way home from church I asked my two-year-old if the teacher had told them a story that morning.

"Yes," she answered.

"What was your story about?"

After a moment of deep thought she proudly announced, "Be quiet!"

Mrs. Warren Haddock, Abilene, Tex.

The Sunday school teacher asked, "Johnny, how do you suppose Lazarus 'came forth' from the grave?"

Without a moment's hesitation Johnny replied with eyes open extra wide, "FAST."

Dennis Wood, Annville, Pa.

Ronnie: "I didn't get to learn my Bible verse last night. My family had to go to the hospital to see my little brother."

Teacher: "Oh, Ronnie, I'm so sorry your brother is sick!"

Ronnie: "He isn't *sick!*"

Teacher: "Was he in an accident? Was he hurt someway?"

Ronnie: "Nope. He's all right."

Teacher: "Then why is he in the hospital?"

Ronnie (with sigh): "Well, he *had* to go there to be *born.*"

Eleanor Weeks, Glendale, Calif.

A kindergarten class had been singing "Be careful little tongue what you say." After the teacher had explained further to the children why it is so hard to control the tongue, a little boy waved his hand for permission to speak:

"I know why it's hard to make the tongue behave. It's because it's in such a slippery place!"

"Lucy's still in Sunday school, singing our duet. I finished first."

First grade teacher: "Dickie, what am I going to do with you? The closing bell has rung and your picture isn't colored, and you don't know your memory verse. I don't suppose you learned a thing today. Now why is that, Dickie?"

Dickie: "Well, you made me sit down and be still and listen, and you *teached* me and *teached* me and *teached* me 'till I couldn't learn anything!"

A little girl was asked by her teacher why she failed to attend her Sunday school class. Came the reply, "Well, I already know how to be better than I am!"

Pauline Tommerdahl, Hendrum, Minn.

The teacher was telling her first graders about Paul appearing before Felix the Governor of Judea and she asked: "Who was Felix?"

"A cat!" answered Billy.

The teacher hastened to correct the situation and explained that Felix was a "governor" or a "ruler."

"Now," said teacher, "Felix was a ruler. What is a ruler?"

Billy again replied in dead seriousness: "A ruler is something you measure with, or get hit with when you are naughty!"

Eleanor Doan, Glendale, California

"I wouldn't mind turning the other cheek, but the bruiser I know concentrates on my chin and nose!"

A third grade boy's interpretation of *A soft answer turneth away wrath: but grievous words stir up anger* (Prov. 15:1):

"It means that if someone gets mad at you, and you don't get mad back at him, he has to go off and be mad by himself. But if someone gets mad at you and you get mad back at him, then you get in a fight!"

Frances Blankenbaker, San Gabriel, Calif.

After Jimmy had attended Sunday school for several weeks his mother asked him how he liked it.

"Oh, I like it fine, but my Sunday school teacher has a very poor memory," replied Jimmy.

"What makes you say that?" mother questioned.

"Because every Sunday she always asks *us* what last week's lesson was about."

Mrs. Pauline Holmes, Scarborough, Ont.

Ilse, a little Jewish refugee girl who had fled Austria with her parents to escape massacre by Hitler's soldiers, was a guest in the home of the Howes, a missionary family in Shanghai. For breakfast one morning Mrs. Howes made waffles, pouring the batter into the iron at the table. Ilse watched wide-eyed, but said nothing. Later, when she rejoined her parents, Ilse's mother asked her what she had for breakfast.

Unhesitatingly Ilse explained, "Mrs. Howes poured milk from a pitcher into a pan and it came out bread!"

Mary Ruth Howes, Waco, Texas

After hearing the Christmas story David asked, "Did the angels sing when I was born too, Mama?"

"No, only when Jesus was born," his mother replied.

To this David thoughtfully responded, "Oh, it's probably because there aren't any shepherds here."

Sam Hofman, Chiapas, Mexico

Ronnie came home from Sunday school after a lesson on Moses in the wilderness. Telling how God had instructed Moses to get water for the Israelites from the rock, he commented, "And Moses must have hit a sewer line, 'cause water went all over the place."

Mrs. Margaret Spencer, Sunland, Calif.

71

A Sunday school teacher suddenly stopped reading a passage in the Bible and asked the youngsters: "Why do you believe in God?"

She got a variety of answers, some full of simple faith, others obviously insincere. The one that stunned her came from the son of a minister. He answered apologetically, "I guess it just runs in our family."

In our Preschool Department the children and teachers sing, "I'm helping, I'm helping, because I love Jesus," as they pick up toys during clean-up time. I found this worked quite well at home, too, with my 2½-year-old Julie—usually. One day, however, I started singing and picking up toys, but noticed that Julie wasn't helping.

I asked her why and she said, "I don't want to—*you* love Jesus, Mommy, *you* pick up toys!"

Mrs. Carolyn Stonacek, Fresno, Calif.

After teaching that Joseph was not Jesus' real father but had been appointed by God to help take care of Mary and the baby, I asked in review, "What do we mean when we say appointed father?" Came the reply, "Well, he was sort of a babysitter father."

Martha Lauber, Limerick, Penna.

"Prince just got himself kicked out of vacation Bible school."

A policeman noticed a boy with a lot of stuff packed on his back riding a tricycle around and around the block. Finally he asked him where he was going.

"I'm running away from home," the boy said.

The policeman then asked him, "Why do you keep going around and around the block?"

The boy answered, "My mother won't let me cross the street."

One cloudy, windy morning two small brothers, three-and-a-half and four-and-a-half years old, stood looking out the window at the clouds as they raced across the sky.

"What makes the clouds move?" asked the younger boy.

After a moment's thought his brother replied, "Why, God and Jesus live up there, and I think they are out walking around."

Mrs. Daniel Stephens, Seattle, Wash.

As Easter drew nearer, we were fortunate to have the chaplain step into our second grade class to give us some insight on the meaning of Lent. In preparation, I asked if anyone knew what Lent was. One pupil answered: "Isn't that the stuff you get on your clothes?"

Miss Anne Steffey, Washington, D.C.

"They were fighting over who made the best angel in the Sunday school play!"

Daddy had just corrected his two-year-old son by saying: "No, Jeff, that's dangerous! If you do that again, I'll spank you!"

Turning to Jeff's sister, Kim, age 3, Daddy attempted to teach a bit of vocabulary: "What does dangerous mean, Kim?"

Kim replied without a moment's hesitation: "You spank!"

Our five-year-old Sally had loved going to nursery class in Sunday school. One day she said she was not going back any more. "But why?" I wanted to know. "You've always loved Sunday school . . ."

"No." She shook her head sadly. "No use going any more. The clay dried out."

Betty Saunders, Oswego, New York

My six-year-old daughter looked on with admiration as I added my 12-year attendance bar to its chain. When she asked if she would ever have that many, I assured her that she probably would, since she already had her third-year pin and I didn't even receive my first pin until I was 11 years old.

She paused in momentary thought and then inquired. "Why, Mommie? Didn't you go into your own class alone until then?"

L. M. Smith, Leaburg, Oregon

Primary child's answer to Old Testament review question: "We have been studying about the Philistines and the satellites."

Clara Wingert, Chambersburg, Pa.

"What is an epistle?" asked the teacher. Billy said, "That's the wife of an apostle."

Faith Shaw, Waterloo, Ia.

The seventh grade lesson dealt with the publican and the sinner. Asked the teacher, "What is a publican?"

Answered one of his wiser students: "The opposite of an 'emocrat."

Ford Dickson, La Canada, Calif.

Kids have
THEIR OWN VERSIONS

Timmy, our pastor's nine-year-old son, was trying to memorize the first chapter of James along with the others who attended prayer meeting. He quoted the first verse without any trouble but he continued on to the second with, "My brethren, count it all joy when you dive into temptation."

Mrs. Jeanne Roth, Sweet Home, Oregon

On a recent test I asked my Sunday school third graders for the name of the man God had saved from the flood.

One eight-year-old enlightened me with: NOAH ZARK.

Esther Lakritz, Beloit, Wisconsin

"And forgive us our debts as we forgive our
dentist."

Mrs. J. E. Holmes, Andover, N.Y.

An errant, but thought-provoking, Scripture quotation by an eight-year-old came out: "If God be for us, you're up against it."

Little Boy: "Didn't God love Adam?"
Teacher: "Yes, of course, why?"
Boy: "Well, we sing 'Jesus Loves Eve'n Me.' "

The boys living next door to us were great on model trains, always adding to their layout. When their younger sister entered my Sunday school class, I heard one little voice in a slightly revised version of the Lord's Prayer: "Forgive us our trestles."

Mrs. T. J. Kleinhaus, Biloxi, Mississippi

Four-year-old version of 23rd Psalm: ". . . he leadeth me beside distilled water."

Mrs. John Lindskoog, Orange, Calif.

A little boy insisted on quoting Matthew 7:20, "By their fruit salad ye shall know them."

Dorothy Jessup, Diagonal, Iowa

Eight-year-old reciting II Tim. 3:17 to memory work teacher: "That we may be perfect, thoroughly varnished unto every good work."

The Rev. Ed Hayes, Denver, Colo.

Our two teen-age sons were monopolizing the supper conversation with a lively discussion about atoms. Eight-year-old Phillip seemed duly impressed with the staggering figures they quoted to "prove" their mathematical wisdom.

With a sagely air he contributed, "Well, years ago, in olden days, at least they had one atom. They had Atom and Eve!"

Mrs. John Peters, Feldbergstrabe, Germany

One of my seven-year-old twins came to me one day and said, "Daddy, when we sin we get smaller, don't we?"

"No," I replied. "Why do you say that?"

"Well," she exclaimed, "the Bible says, 'All have sinned and come short!' "

Mr. Richard Jacobsen, Norwalk, Calif.

During a pictured review of the story of baby Moses, the teacher asked a class of kindergarteners:

"When sister Miriam came out from her hiding place, what did she ask the princess, who was holding little baby Moses?"

Bill's hand shot up, and the teacher called for his answer. It came in revised, modern language:

"Do you want a baby-sitter?"

Marie Chapman, Goodlettsville, Tenn.

Nine-year-old boy memorizing 23rd Psalm: "And I shall duel in the house of the Lord forever."

James R. Baisley, Lynbrook, N.Y.

Our seven-year-old son was highly impressed when his eighteen-year-old brother was drafted. A couple weeks later he was overheard singing . . .

"Stand up, stand up for Jesus
Ye soldiers of Ft. Bliss . . ."

Rosalie Keller, San Bernardino, Calif.

The teacher of a Bible club in Portland, Oregon, was teaching a group of Negro children James 1:5, *If any of you lack wisdom, let him ask of God . . .*

"What does it mean to *lack* something, boys and girls?" she asked. One boy enthusiastically raised his hand.

"Well," he answered. "If you 'lack' somebody, you just lack 'em, that's all—'cause they's yo' friend!"

Margie Cross, Portland, Oregon

After teaching the verse, *Draw nigh to God, and He will draw nigh to you,* (James 4:8) to a mission class of children who had very little previous training, I asked if someone would like to quote it for me.

I received an immediate response from the little boy whom I had least expected to recite. He stood up and said clearly, "Draw a knife on God and He will draw a knife on you."

Mrs. W. Z. Rose, Ray, Ariz.

A nine-year-old girl in a Mississippi church, participating in a Baptist Training Union, was asked: "Why were the deacons chosen?"

She said, "To take care of the windows and organs."

Evangelical Press News Service

Little Danny was reciting Isaiah 26:3, which reads in part, *Thou wilt keep him in perfect peace* . . . Danny's version was: "Thou wilt keep him in perfect shape."

Mrs. W. D. Clark, Riverside, Calif.

A Sunday school teacher reported that the excuse of a little girl for not having her memory work was "because the only copy of the Bible we have at home is the reversed version."

The kindergarten teacher spent the morning telling her pupils about Jesus' stilling of the waters. Throughout the lesson she emphasized the memory verse, and at closing time she asked if anyone could repeat it for her.

John, a wiggly, noisy little boy, said very emphatically, "Please be still."

Mrs. Emily Payton, Yerington, Neb.

My wife was teaching some of her students the meaning of the Apostles' Creed. After considerable lecturing, she gave them a little quiz. Each student was asked to write the creed as well as he could remember it.

"I believe in God," wrote one, "and in His only forgotten son."

Henry E. Leabo, Tennessee Colony, Texas

Betty was supposed to learn a new Bible verse at Sunday school each week. One Sunday her parents asked what she had learned. Whether drawing from experience or not, she managed to fit together this Scriptural jigsaw:

"A lie is an abomination unto the Lord—and—and—a very present help in time of trouble."

Marion Fulton, Jacksonville, Fla.

The teacher was giving a chalk talk to illustrate Matthew 5:16: *Let your light so shine before men* . . . He drew a picture of a light bulb with rays shining from it, then asked the class what it meant.

A little boy answered, "It means to let your light bulb shine."

Mrs. C. D. Skinner, Dallas, Texas

I was teaching my class of five-year-olds the memory verse, *O come, let us worship him.* I asked the group, "Who knows what 'worship' means?" After a moment's thought Ronny answered, "I should know what it means. I hear it every day when my mommy gets dinner ready and says, 'Ronny, go to the bathroom and worsh-up.'"

Etta King, Manteca, Calif

Our custom during the Junior Department opening worship was to have a standing hymn, prayer, and then have each student quote a verse of Scripture before sitting down.

On one occasion all had recited a verse except nine-year-old Peter who shifted his weight from one foot to the other, trying to think of a verse. The superintendent tried to help by suggesting various references, but to no avail. Suddenly Peter's eyes lit up, and standing tall he said, "Thou shalt not smoke!"

Frederic W. Moler, Pittsburgh, Pa.

Kids have ideas
ABOUT PRAYER

As I concluded the lesson on praying. I asked one of my primaries, "John, why don't you send a message to God tonight before you go to bed?"

He replied, "Sure, what's His address?"

Eugene Norris, Columbus, Ohio

I overheard one of my Primary teachers comparing prayer to a two-way telephone with God. Little Tommy, who had been chattering off and on all morning, looked up suddenly and said, "You mean I can call up God?"

"No, I don't think so, Tommy," the teacher responded. "I think your line is out of order this morning!"

Mr. and Mrs. Alan Packer, Greenville, Ill.

A tiny four-year-old was spending a night away from home. At bedtime, she knelt at her hostess' knee to say her prayers, expecting the usual prompting.

Finding Mrs. B. unable to help her, she concluded. "Please, God, 'scuse me. I can't remember my prayers, and I'm staying with a lady who don't know any."

Reported version of "table grace" by three-year-old girl:

"You are all right, God. Thank you for this food. Amen please."

Mrs. H. S. Bledsoe, Marshfield, Mo.

Prayer of a young child: "Bless Mother and Daddy . . . and dear God, take awful good care of Yourself because if anything happens to You we're sunk."

A junior high boy was heard to pray in Sunday school, "Dear Lord, bless this offering. No, this is not the offering. I don't know what it is. I had better sit down. Amen."

Paul is two-and-a-half years old. His mother has taught him to say, when leaving the table, "May I please be excused?"

She is also teaching him a little prayer to say before meals:

"Come, Lord Jesus, be our guest,
May these gifts to us be blest."

One day he said the blessing as follows:

"Come, Lord Jesus, be our guest, and
May I please be excused?"

Florence Long, Long Beach, Calif.

Mike was late Sunday morning and so he prayed, "Dear God, don't let me be late for Sunday school."

Then Mike stumbled and fell down. As he picked himself up, he said, "Dear God, I want to be on time, but please don't push me."

Lillian R. Lawrence, San Bruno, Calif.

Five-year-old Jan likes long prayers, probably to forestall bedtime. She says, "Jesus, bless Daddy and Mother. Bless everybody in the church. Bless everybody in the whole world."

The other night, however, after a moment's hesitation, she added, ". . . *and everybody in outer space.*"

Mrs. J. C. Rainey, Des Moines, Iowa

One week, six-year-old Richard's father was called out of state to preach. During daily devotions, Richard's mother heard him pray, ". . . and bless my father in whatever state he is in."

Lucy D. Caruso, Los Angeles, Calif.

Five-year-old Kathie had a habit of making long drawn-out bedtime prayers. On one occasion her mother, thinking to shorten them, said, "Amen" during a slight pause. Kathie prayed on. Again her mother suggested, "Amen."

Then Kathie said, "God, don't pay any attention to her. She doesn't know when I'm done."

The prayer was continued.

Mrs. Freda B. Elliott, Ashland, Oregon

Kids have ideas
ABOUT HEAVEN

I had just finished telling my four-year-old son about Jesus and heaven. He went out to play, but in a few minutes he came running into the house, crying. "Mama, Mama, Come quick! Here comes heaven and Jesus is in it!"

I ran out and looked up. He had seen a big white blimp!

Mrs. Clara Fuller, Los Angeles, Calif.

A discussion of heaven with the boys and girls in children's church brought to light a hitherto unexplored advantage when four-year-old Becky said, "We won't have to take naps when we get there!"

Irene Royce, White Lake, Wis.

After hearing a lesson on Jesus, the Good Shepherd, a "cowboy minded" four-year-old boy replied, "I am glad God made me because when I get to heaven I can ride His donkey and herd His sheep, and all He'll have to do is *cook!*"

Freeman Taylor, Valentine, Neb.

94

Seven-year-old Jimmy was thinking about heaven. His conclusion: "I think going to heaven is like a little puppy playing in a new back yard."

One Sunday when I was serving as a primary superintendent, the pupils and I started talking about what a wonderful place heaven is. Different pupils chimed in with what they thought they knew about heaven. As we all started to enjoy our anticipation of heaven, a little fellow in the front row remarked in a loud and thoroughly homesick voice, "Just like Texas!"

Mrs. Margaret Pocta, San Diego, Calif.

The four-year-olds listened attentively to their VBS teacher describe heaven. One little fellow listened to all the wonders of it, cradled his cheek thoughtfully in his hand and said: "I 'fink' I'll take a two-week vacation there."

Mrs. Harold Boadway, Breslau, Ontario, Can.

I asked my kindergarten class, "Does anyone know what an angel is?"

One little girl said, "I know." So I asked her, "What?"

She looked up at me with her big blue eyes and answered, "God—dressed up!"

Naomi Cray, Richmond, Me.

Kids have ideas
ABOUT GOD

It was a particularly beautiful autumn day and our order of worship included the singing of the hymn, "This Is My Father's World." Midway through it I felt my four-year-old Danny tugging at my sleeve.

"This *is not* Daddy's world, is it?" came a loud whisper accompanied by the triumphant look of one who's discovered an error.

I hastily shook my head and later in the afternoon had a talk with my son about the difference between our "Daddy" and our Heavenly Father.

Mrs. Kathryn Sommers, Tecumseh, Michigan

Our pastor was a very large man who said the Lord had given him a "great understanding," glancing down at his size 14 shoes as he said it. One Sunday morning he left his galoshes inside the door of the Sunday school to drain. A few moments later I found two of my kindergarteners crouched beside those gigantic boots, their eyes the size of tennis balls. One of them looked up at me and whispered, "Are those God's galoshes?"

Mrs. Marion Fulton, Jacksonville, Florida

Grandma read aloud from Genesis to her little granddaughter. After she had finished, the child seemed lost in thought. "Well, dear, what do you think of it?" Grandma asked.

"Oh, I just love it," the child replied. "You never know what God is going to do next!"

Mildred Cook, Los Angeles, Calif.

"What makes the lightning? Does Jesus have a flashlight?"

Mrs. W. D. Clark, *Riverside, Calif.*

98

A television announcer was interviewing a six-year-old and queried, "Do you know where God is?" The youngster's omniscient answer was prompt: "Do you know where He isn't?"

A five-year-old lad kept shooting his pop gun at the sky and explained, "I'm shooting God down out of heaven." When asked why, he answered defiantly, "I don't want Him watching me all the time."

The conversation coming home on the Sunday school bus was getting quite theological for four-, five- and six-year-olds. The fact that God never had a beginning had stirred quite a furor. Matters came to a climax when a small boy exploded with the loud and frantic query, "But where did He get His-self?"

The Rev. Ellwood Munger, Los Angeles, Calif.

One night after prayers and our good-night kiss to our young son I was surprised to see the light in his room flick back on.

I called in to ask if anything were wrong and he replied, "No, Mom, but I have something private to say to God and I need the light on so he'll know it's me."

Nadene M. Murphy, Valemount, B.C.

"Dear God, we had a good time at church today. I wish you could have been there."

Mrs. Evelyn Pickering, Calhoun City, Miss.

Five-year-old Billy was riding in the car with all the family. Suddenly he kissed the air with a loud "smack!"

"That's for Jesus," he said. "He's here but I can't see Him so I just kissed the air."

Mrs. Wm. T. Greig Jr., Glendale, Calif.

After a particularly hectic day with my two-year-old, I took him on my lap and asked, "David, don't you love Mommy?"

"No!" came his quick reply, but after seeing my crestfallen face, he smiled, patted my cheek and said, "but Jesus loves you."

Mrs. A. W. Thomas, Anaheim, Calif.

This past summer we took our first airplane trip. When we had gained altitude enough to fly among the clouds, our four-year-old, Steven, said, "I hope we don't bump into Jesus."

Mrs. R. V. Gittings, Kansas City, Mo.

I did not think my three-year-old son was absorbing much in his Sunday school class until one day I scolded him for being bad. I told him I did not like him when he was naughty. He sulked for a moment, then said, "That's okay! Jesus loves me!"

Mrs. J. W. Melton, Jr., San Francisco, Calif.

Kids have ideas
ABOUT SIN AND THE DEVIL

Five-year-old Nancy had been naughty and an ominous silence hung over the dinner table. Tension only increased when Nancy ventured, "I know why we are naughty."

Demanded irate mother, "Just why?"

Remembering what she'd learned in VBS Nancy explained, "Because that little girl gave an apple to that little boy."

Paul M. McKowen, Canon Beach, Ore.

My third-graders were discussing how difficult it is sometimes not to tease, not to argue, not to be sassy. For a week they had kept track of things they had done which they really should not have done. Although the lists were private and not even to be brought to school, Robert had none. "I didn't really do anything," he explained. "Things just kept happening to me."

Mrs. T. J. Kleinhaus, Biloxi, Miss.

Daddy had just finished reading family devotions and Mary (age 4) had prayed, too.

Mark (a 6th-grader) turned to Mother and asked, "Does God hear Mary's prayers?" Mark was assured that God did, but he replied, "I didn't think God heard sinners' prayers."

Daddy proceeded to explain about Mary's tender age, God's love, the age of responsibility, etc. As he was finishing, Mary cut in, "Yeah, that's right. I'm not a sinner yet, but I will be when I get older!"

Mrs. Don Thimsen, Minneapolis, Minn.

I was teaching my nursery class that God sees us and watches over us at all times. I taught them to say together, "God sees me when I'm good; God sees me when I'm naughty." Then I questioned them.

"Sheila, does God see you when you are good?"

"Yes."

"Does God see you when you are naughty?"

"No."

"But Sheila . . ." I began.

"I'm not naughty," finished Sheila.

Mrs. Freda B. Elliott, Corona, Calif.

A lively six-year-old boy, when corrected by the teacher as his class marched into the church sanctuary, presented this original alibi:

"Well, that old devil is so fast that he has me doing the wrong thing before I know it."

Sydney H. Cooke, Vancouver, B.C.

One evening my neighbor's little boy was sent to bed because of being so naughty. The little boy knelt to pray and his mother said he should ask God to make him a better boy. He prayed accordingly, and near the end he said, "But don't worry if you can't, God, because I'm having a good time the way I am."

Mrs. June Smith, Ripon, Wis.

The visiting evangelist taught our Sunday schoolers that one of God's commands is *Thou shalt not steal* (Exodus 20:15). To illustrate the lesson he pointed out that taking cookies from the cookie jar without asking is stealing.

That afternoon one family discussed this lesson, and someone recalled the illustration about taking cookies. "Yes," a little boy replied, "but he didn't say anything about raisins."

Mrs. I. M. Wolgemuth, Mt. Joy, Pa.

A Primary teacher was trying to tell about the devil without frightening her students.

"He'll trip you up every chance he gets," she warned. "Whenever he can, he makes you sin. He *lies* to you. He surely is not your friend. Why," she concluded, "he doesn't even *like* you."

"That suits *me* fine," responded an eight-year-old. "I don't like *him* either."

Mrs. Ruth Peterman, Minneapolis, Minn.

Kids reflect
WHAT THEY THINK

When I asked my class what they were thankful for, one little boy replied, "My glasses." Then he explained, "They keep the boys from fighting me and the girls from kissing me."

Mrs. L. J. Workman, Wichita, Kansas

Preacher's son to little friend while watching a ball game: "My daddy knows all about God. He's got a book on Him!"

Douglas Rambo, Madison, Tenn.

"I'm worried! I'm beginning to like girls better than my lizard collection!"

When the offering plate was passed during church services, small Douglas hesitantly opened a tight fist and parted with his coin. Looking up at his mother, he whispered, "Some of these days I'm coming in here for nothing!"

Bonnie Braun, Cincinnati, Ohio

The teacher of a class of young boys asked them to tell the meaning of loving kindness.

One pupil replied, "If I was hungry and someone gave me a piece of bread and butter, that would be kindness. But if they put lots of jam on it, that would be loving kindness."

A four-year-old daughter demanded that her father read the story of the baby Moses night after night. Finally the father tape-recorded the story. When she asked for the story he switched on the recorder.

This was fine for several nights. Then one evening the little girl pushed the story book at her father.

"Now honey," he said, "you know how to turn on the recorder."

"Yes," she replied, "But I can't sit on its lap."

After our Cadet (age 9-13) camp, a Sunday school teacher asked his class of boys, "What is counseling?"

One of his students replied, "I know! It's threatening!"

The Rev. Bruce Donham, Anderson, Ind.

In writing an essay a student in the fourth grade wrote, "The trouble with parents is that when we get them they are so old that they are very hard to change."

Our six-year-old girl was asked to sing a special missionary song at the VBS closing program. "I'm singing 'Jesus Loves Me' in Chinese," she told us eagerly, "and the rest of the kids are going to hum in American."

Mrs. Michael McCourt, Alderwood Manor, Wash.

"Here's my report card—and I'm tired of watching TV anyway."

Our four-year-old Keith was listening attentively to his two older brothers reminisce about events that had occurred before Keith arrived in the family. "Where was I?" Keith asked.

"You weren't even born yet," said James loftily.

"Yeah, where *were* you, anyway?" teased Peter.

Keith thought for a moment, then replied simply, "I was still with God."

Mrs. James M. Dolliver, Olympia, Washington

Teacher: "Today I shall tell you a Bible story on Moses and the plagues sent on the people of Egypt. Does anyone know what a plague is?"

Six-year-old girl: "Yes, my brother is one."

Mrs. Pauline R. York, Winston-Salem, N.C.

Snow was falling as the children arrived for Junior Action Group. At prayer time many children participated, thanking God for His goodness, asking His help for sick relatives and friends, seeking His guidance for their leaders.

When Ken's turn came, he prayed straight from the heart: "Thank you, God, for letting it snow so we won't have to go to school tomorrow."

Kids reflect
WHAT THEY LEARN

Five-year-old Johnny came home from school one day and reported that he had to stand in the hall for an hour. Mother asked him why and he explained, "Well, all I did was start shouting 'Praise the Lord!' like one of the men at church!"

Mrs. Betty Bailey, Laingsburg, Mich.

Our little neighbor boy came in while a minister was preaching on the radio. He listened for a moment, then said, "He's talking about Jesus. Our radio doesn't talk about Jesus."

Carmen Funkhouser, Lancaster, Pa.

"Only 48 more Sundays and I get my one-year pin . . ."

"I like Christmas time—especially Christmas Day," said Tommy thoughtfully. "There's so much to think about. I wish I had been born on Christmas Day, like Jesus was."

Carol's answer was emphatic: "Jesus wasn't born on Christmas Day! He was born on a regular day. But it became Christmas because He was born that day. Before then it wasn't Christmas at all. Now it's Christmas everywhere! Don't you see? He makes it Christmas!"

"But it isn't Christmas everywhere," Tommy disagreed. "Some places don't have Christmas. Can you imagine a place without Christmas?"

"It can be Christmas even if places don't have it," Carol reasoned. "People can have Christmas. When Jesus lives in your heart He makes it Christmas!"

Miss Eleanor Doan, Glendale, Calif.

Pointing to an unusually bright star one evening shortly after Christmas, a neighbor's four-year-old son asked, "Mommy, is Mary going to have another baby?"

Annie Laurie VanTungeln, Tulsa, Oklahoma

While teaching a class of juniors in children's church, I asked what they thought "longsuffering" meant. One little girl replied, "Doesn't that have something to do with marriage?"

Robert L. Wilbur, Mt. Vernon, Ohio

"And remember, class—if any of you are ever confronted with perplexing problems or soul-searching questions, please feel free to see me for personal counseling."

The pastor had preached a sermon on the kinds of love mentioned in the Bible—AGAPE, the highest form of unselfish love, shown by God when He gave His Son; PHILOS, friendly or brotherly love; EROS, sensual love.

The next day one of the mothers from the church had to discipline her junior. In great disgust the youngster told his mother, "You're not even showing me PHILOS love!"

Ginny Wells, Irving, Texas

When my little daughter, age four, started to nursery school, one of the first things she learned was matching up pairs of different kinds. There were in the class identical twin girls, and Kelly enjoyed playing with them. I asked her about her new friends, and she replied, "Mom, I sure do like those matching girls."

Sharon Carpenter, Panorama City, Calif.

The pastor, talking to juniors about the universality of sin, told how Adam became a sinner and how those born after Adam were born sinners. To illustrate, he cited examples from the animal world: birds have little birds, cats have kittens, bears have bear cubs. Then he asked, "What do dogs have?" expecting the answer, "Puppies or little dogs." Instead, a little fellow shot back the first word that came to his mind: "Fleas!"

Rev. Richard Claar, Branson, Mo.

"Say 'Our class won the attendance banner'—not 'We murdered them.'"

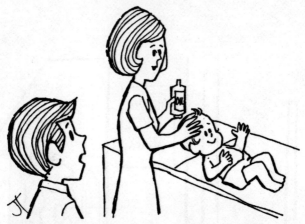

Eight-year-old David was watching mother oil baby brother's scalp. David questioned, "Why are you doing that, Mother. Is Peter going to be a king?"

Mrs. W. Rust, Sheboygan, Wis.

One rather warm afternoon I had several errands to do and had my two little boys with me. They had been sitting in their car seats for quite a while and were getting restless and bored, and started to pick on each other. Craig was two and a half, and Brian was a year and a half. I was too hot and tired to put up with this, so I stopped the car and really scolded them in a voice that didn't hide my irritation. When I was finished, Craig turned and looked out the car window singing, "Jesus loves me, this I know . . ."

Mary Ann Lamascus, Downey, Calif.

Kids reflect
THE TIMES in which they live

On the second day of VBS the preschool teacher was preparing to tell the Bible story. As she placed on the flannelboard the same background used the day before, a five-year-old boy exclaimed, "Oh, it's a rerun."

Mrs. Jack Rink, Churchville, Pennsylvania

Sunday school saga resulting from TV commercial influences:

Two four-year-olds in class . . . SHE is busy putting on her lipstick, which she brought from home . . . HE is leaning over to her and saying, "Smell of my hair. I have on some Brylcreem. After church is over, you can pursue me" . . . To which SHE agreed . . . Teacher at wits end.

Mrs. J. D. Brewen, Pine Bluffs, Wyo.

119

Many of our primary pupils often arrive 15 minutes early for Sunday night Christian Endeavor. During this period they work industriously on various projects and handwork. One Sunday they were busily engaged in pre-session cutting and pasting when the regular 6:00 P.M. bell rang loudly to signal the beginning of the meeting. One small voice promptly called out, "Coffee Break!"

Frances Blankenbaker, San Gabriel, Calif.

The Kindergarten Superintendent was taking advantage of the warmer weather as she led the children on a tour of the church grounds to look for "signs of spring."

Soon little John, the son of the pastor, called out, "Here is a sign of spring!" Everyone turned to look. John was pointing to an old Dairy Queen container.

Mrs. Myra Trude, Minnetonka, Minn.

Teaching the Books of the Bible to seven-year-olds means a lot of repetition. One week the children recited them as I put the individual names on the flannelboard. As I placed "Judges," I said, "Now what comes after Judges?"

One of our brighter boys answered gravely, "Policemen!"

Mrs. Thos. Carlton, Philadelphia, Pa.

120

"First Church doesn't usually give letters for its Sunday school, but if you want one that badly . . ."

My lesson to the nursery class was about Christ healing a sick boy. Pathetically I told them, "Mother didn't know what to do. Father didn't know what to do. What do you suppose they did?"

Little Jeanne answered promptly, "They gave him a shot!"

Betty Wildt, Stockton, Calif.

Long before my husband and I started going to church and Sunday school, we made the children go every Sunday. Every Sunday we gave them a dime for the offering. The amount never changed. We had some relatives come to visit us from the east and they had a little boy the age of our boy. Shannon wanted his cousin to come to Sunday school with him. After giving a list of reasons why his cousin should be allowed to come, he ended with, "And besides, it only costs a dime."

Georgia Morton, Pacoima, Calif.

When my wife, a Sunday school teacher, enrolled in a local college for a theology course that would help with her teaching, it immediately interested our ten-year-old, Mark.

"Mom," he asked, "are you going out for cheerleader?"

Henry E. Leabo, Tennessee Colony, Texas

During our memory time, I asked the primaries to look up the verse in their Bibles. Marvin didn't understand the Bible reference. Fumbling through the pages of his Bible, he turned to the boy next to him and said, "What was that *channel* again?"

Mrs. Ethan Mazaraki, Fort Wayne, Ind

"Excuse me, Sir, but how much farther is it to Sunday school?"